# Tam Met Reb

By Sally Cowan

Tam sat in the pit.

Tam met Reb.

Reb has a cap.

It has a rip.

Tam can see a rat!

It is Rib.

Rib is a pet rat.

Reb has a bat.

Tam and Reb hit and hit!

Reb can see Rib!

Rib is in the pit.

Reb and Tam pat Rib.

Pat, pat, pat.

# CHECKING FOR MEANING

1. Where did Tam meet Reb? *(Literal)*

2. What pet does Reb have? *(Literal)*

3. Why do you think Tam and Reb played with the bat? *(Inferential)*

# EXTENDING VOCABULARY

| | |
|---|---|
| **sat** | Look at the word *sat*. What other words do you know that rhyme with *sat*? |
| **rip** | What does the word *rip* mean in the story? What other word could be used that has the same meaning? |
| **bat** | What is another meaning of the word *bat*, other than the bat used to hit with? |

## MOVING BEYOND THE TEXT

1. How do you think Tam and Reb feel about their new friendship?

2. What other animals do you think make good pets? Why?

3. What would Reb need to do to care for Rib?

4. Do you think Tam and Reb will be good friends? Why?

## SPEED SOUNDS

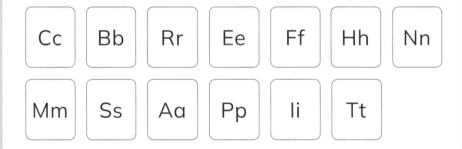

| Cc | Bb | Rr | Ee | Ff | Hh | Nn |
|----|----|----|----|----|----|----|
| Mm | Ss | Aa | Pp | Ii | Tt | |

# PRACTICE WORDS

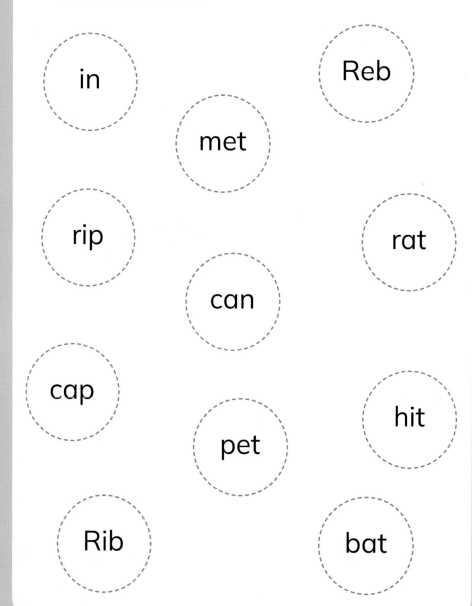

in

Reb

met

rip

rat

can

cap

hit

pet

Rib

bat